Alive Aware Awake

Living an Ordinary Sacred Life

Mary J Welch

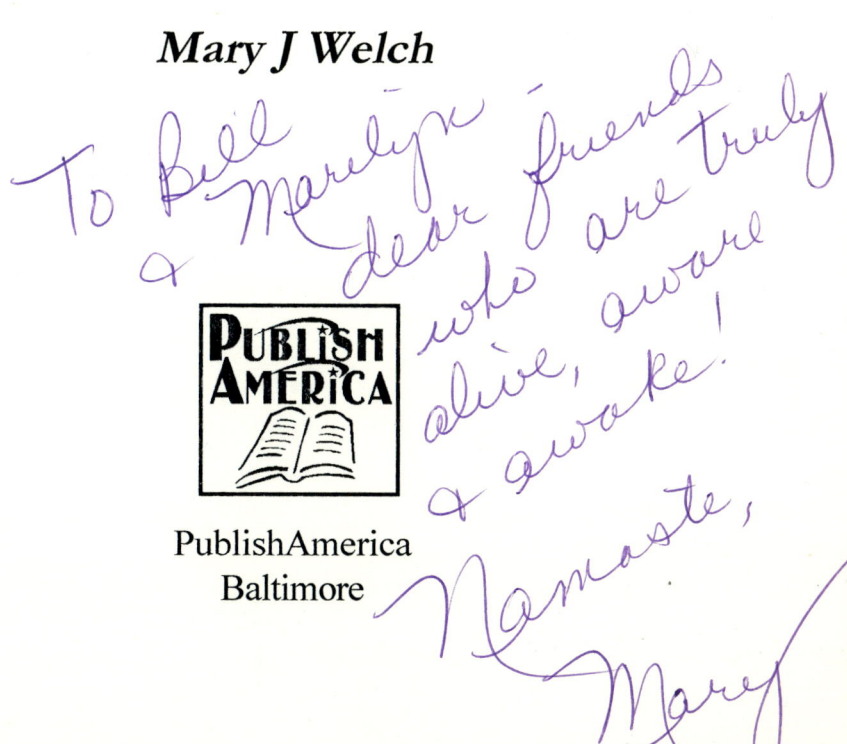

PublishAmerica
Baltimore

© 2009 by Mary J Welch.
All rights reserved. No part of this book may be reproduced, stored in a retrieval system or transmitted in any form or by any means without the prior written permission of the publishers, except by a reviewer who may quote brief passages in a review to be printed in a newspaper, magazine or journal.

First printing

This publication contains the opinions and ideas of its author. Author intends to offer information of a general nature. Any reliance on the information herein is at the reader's own discretion.

The author and publisher specifically disclaim all responsibility for any liability, loss, or right, personal or otherwise, which is incurred as a consequence, directly or indirectly, of the use and application of any contents of this book. They further make no representations or warranties with respect to the accuracy or completeness of the contents of this work and specifically disclaim all warranties including without limitation any implied warranty of fitness for a particular purpose. Any recommendations are made without any guarantee on the part of the author or the publisher.

ISBN: 1-60703-365-8
PUBLISHED BY PUBLISHAMERICA, LLLP
www.publishamerica.com
Baltimore

Printed in the United States of America

Dedicated to

Rachael Renee
My beloved infant granddaughter
whose very brief, but brilliant life
continues to light up my life with miracles!

Preface

This book is my story. It's about my human journey as a spiritual being and the struggles and joys of waking up to the essential truth of my divinity. It is a personal sharing of insights and "aha" moments that came from reflecting on everyday life experiences and from listening to the quiet gentle voice within me.

This book is also an invitation. It is an invitation for you to tell your story and learn its lessons so you can free yourself from the story and embrace the truth of who you are.

At the level of our soul, this book is about you and me. It's about honoring ourselves and each other as a unique manifestation of a life force energy ~ a sacred expression of *Spirit*.

Contents

Acknowledgments 9
Introduction 13

Chapter 1: Sacred Spaces 17
Chapter 2: Natural Conversations 20
Chapter 3: The Small Universe 23
Chapter 4: Oceans of Insights 29
Chapter 5: Gifts from Mother 34
Chapter 6: Underneath It All 38
Chapter 7: The Awe in God 49

Afterword 60
Praise for the Retreat 62
Wisdom Resources 63
About the Author 65

Acknowledgments

I am deeply grateful to the following people for their presence in my life:

First and most especially, Mike, my very best friend and my husband of more than forty years. Every day he teaches me how to love more deeply by his example of living the truth that unconditional love is a choice.

Our daughters, Katy, Bridget, and Michelle, who each in their own way are mirrors for me and are teaching me to love what is and be my authentic self. Their love and admiration sustains my passion for staying awake to the truth of my being.

Our granddaughters, Emily, Sara, Mickaela, and Isabel, who have brought delight and joy into our home and for whom I am forever grateful they were born.

Our grandsons, Erik, Zachary, Colin, and Trevor, who tease me, make me laugh, and teach me the importance of being a playful adult.

Our sons-in-law, Jon, Jeff, and John, whose integrity and generosity are gifts that strengthen our family bond of love and commitment.

My mom, Jane, who said yes to birthing me and whose example taught me how to be a loving spiritual being.

My dad, Art, whose respect for me and his trust in my abilities encouraged me to be who I truly am, a leader and a seeker of wisdom.

My sisters, Kathy, Anne, Barbara, Julia, Teresa, and Bridget, who continue to teach me what it means to celebrate the diversity of women.

My mother-in-law, Dottie, who raised a son to love a strong woman and whose example of independence fed my own desires.

My father-in-law, Earl, who taught his son to honor women and who delighted in my gullibility.

The many male friends I have been blessed with, especially my brothers, Mark, Phil, Tim, Tony, and Chris; as well as Earnie, Steve, and Ray, who invited me to open my mind, stretch my boundaries, and embrace the unknown.

And lastly, my profound gratitude to all my magnificent women friends, especially my dearest friend, Mary M. Each one of you has made a lasting impression on my soul and you have helped me see more clearly the beauty and privilege of being a spiritual being having a human experience as a woman.

I Am Alive, Aware, and Awake!
© Hiram Titus

I am alive, aware and awake,
I am alive, aware and awake,
Joyous and enthusiastic for life!
I am alive, aware and awake,
I am alive, aware and awake,
Joyous and enthusiastic for life!

I see each morning as a new beginning,
I greet each day as an opportunity to share,
I'm breathing deep and I feel connected
To all the love expressing everywhere!

I am alive, aware and awake,
I am alive, aware and awake,
Joyous and enthusiastic for life!
I am alive, aware and awake,
I am alive, aware and awake,
Joyous and enthusiastic,
Joyous and enthusiastic,
Joyous and enthusiastic for life!

Introduction

I fell in love with the song *I Am Alive, Aware and Awake!* by Hiram Titus the very first time I heard it. It sparks a surge of positive energy within me whenever I sing it and it also causes me to ask myself the question, "Am I really alive, aware and awake at this moment?" Sometimes the answer is a feeble "no," but often it is a resounding "yes!"

The first time I asked the question I wasn't even sure of the distinctions between the words. I often used them, but not interchangeably; so I chose to spend time reflecting on their specific meaning to me. What I discovered is that they are a new way for me to look at an ancient way of looking at myself. They describe the trinity of who I am, *body, mind, and soul.*

The search to uncover the truth of my spiritual self has included learning how these three aspects of myself are separate, yet one in the unique expression of who I am. It is my soul that intuitively longs for wholeness and it is my soul that knows I am already whole and one with all of creation. It is my mind that grasps the scientific concept that we are all of one source energy and it is my mind that argues with that concept. It is my body that resonates with the truth that we are all connected and it is my body that feels tired of trying to connect. In those brief moments when the knowing and the feeling occur simultaneously, I feel alive, aware, and awake. And in those moments, I believe my ordinary life shines brighter as a sacred light into the world.

This has not been a simple discovery. I traipsed down several paths, encountering many obstacles and many exhilarating experiences before I claimed this truth of oneness of body, mind, and soul with all of creation.

Some of that journey is shared in these pages. My thoughts and experiences are framed by the distinctions of alive, aware and awake; but they are also framed by my belief that the search to uncover my spiritual self involves being consciously open to the mystery of nature, my body, my subconscious, my creativity, and to the mystery of spirit.

Even though this book is neatly divided into three parts, know that my experiences are not so clearly categorized. My life is not that simple. All three aspects of my trinity are interwoven with the mysteries in every part of my story. Organizing did bring clarity however, and that created space for insights to emerge from the confusing, jumbled thoughts and experiences of my life.

I encourage you to allow my experiences and my insights to be the catalyst for reflecting on your own experiences. If you choose to do the activities at the end of each section, take your time. Create a sacred space where you can journal and allow the wisdom of your essence to gently speak to you and permeate every cell in your body.

I don't have the right answers; I have only my questions and my answers. Your questions and your answers are unique to you. Honor both the commonness of our experiences and the differences, and trust that whatever insights you receive from reading my story will be perfectly timed for you.

I still have much discovering to do and many more moments of serend!p!tous insights ahead. By staying fully alive in my surroundings, aware of who I think I am, and awake to the truth of who I really am, I feel confident I will continue to live an ordinary sacred life that is extraordinary.

Alive in the Mystery of the Universe

*…You are a child of the universe,
no less than the trees and the stars, you have a right to be here,
and whether or not it is clear to you, no doubt the universe is unfolding as it should.*
Desiderata. Max Ehrman

Chapter 1
Sacred Spaces

How do you get your mind around a concept that seems incomprehensible, like space? I have been in awe of the vastness of outer space for many years, but until very recently, I could not even vaguely grasp the reality of it. However, not long ago, through a mundane visual experience, my perception of "space" was transformed serend!p!tously!

On a bright, blue sky, very cold winter day, I was vacuuming in my family room. The sun was shining through the windows, creating a perfectly distinct sunbeam from the window to the fireplace, and in the dazzling light I could see the gazillions of tiny dust particles I had stirred up. Each one was completely separate from the other, floating in a space that was minuscule compared to the size of the area of my family room and almost negligible as I gradually widened my view to include the space extending out into the brilliant blue sky. There seemed to be no physical connection among the tiny particles, yet they were obviously part of a greater totality. I stood transfixed over this celestial display and found myself reflecting on how this image of the dust particles against the backdrop of outer space is a great metaphor for the mysteries of the cosmos and the mystery of "inner" sacred space. I honestly saw the "no-thing-ness" between particles and yet I knew without a shadow of a doubt that there was "something" holding them together, something that had a power greater than any personal power of my own. I felt awed and excited by the simplicity and the complexity of this natural occurrence.

I then walked through the display of sunlit dust particles and looked at it from another angle. There was no apparent change in the sunbeam or particles, but my perception certainly changed! Standing in the way of the light caused me to see less of the particles and less of the whole. I thought about all of the dust particles I wasn't even seeing because they were in the shadow, not in the path of the sunlight. This was a clear metaphor for what happens to me when my vision is clouded by my fears and I refuse to see things from more than one perspective. The whole experience took only a couple of minutes, but my belief in the reality of the unseen was affirmed and I felt a renewed determination to keep my eyes open for profound insights from unexpected places.

Believe me, this wasn't the first time I had seen a galaxy of dust mites in my home, but it sure was the first time I experienced a spiritual moment with them. My family room had become a sacred space because I had my eyes open to seeing something familiar through a new lens. That can happen anywhere and we can create it at will, we don't have to wait for a serend!p!tous happening. Sacred spaces happen when there is a conscious intention to be more aware of the beauty and mystery surrounding us and within us.

When I am in touch with the sacred space within me, my personal life is more fulfilling and I am more effective as a retreat facilitator and coach. I am able to honor the sacred space within a person or a group only when I honor it within myself. By taking the time to know the essence of myself, I model what I expect of others and together, we reflect the beauty within each of us and grow deeper in our awareness of the sacred. Then we can stand in awe—just as I stood in awe of the dust cloud.

Here are some ways I stay awake to the sacred space within and around me. Consider how you can use this list to add to or refresh your experiences of the sacred everywhere. To experience sacred space:

Light a candle. That's all, simply light a candle and know that by doing so you have enfolded whatever you are doing in the sacred warmth and light of awareness.

Be still. Turn off the radio, the television and the chatter in your head chanting the "to-do" list. Listen to your inner voice and honor that sound as a sacred sound, no matter what it says. Observe it from a neutral perspective and befriend it. It has much to teach.

Listen to music that is soothing and healing. Relax and open your heart. Pay attention to the words and allow them to sink into your very being .

Do the personal growth work needed to become aware of your sacred center. Choose courage instead of fear and freedom will be your gift.

Define for yourself what is "sacred space."

Work in circles. Notice circles. Create circles…wherever you go. They are the perfect container for expressing the truth of our lives.

Actively participate in a community that expresses its appreciation for the sacred.

Declare your intention to be aware of the sacredness in the mundane and to expect the unexpected!

Make time for spiritual renewal a priority in your life. When you return to the everyday happenings in your life, you will have a new perspective and the sacredness of your life will have a brighter glow.

Be mindful. Embrace what's happening right *now*. Your body is breathing, the planet is spinning, the birds are singing, the mail is being delivered. Be grateful—a divine order is at work.

There is no need to reach beyond the stars to find a sacred space. It is here, right now, in this place, wherever we are. Our whole life is sacred—the planet on which we live, the bodies in which we move and love, the people who share our life journey, our past experiences, this present moment, and the future we are creating today. They are all sacred, we need only see them through eyes of awe.

Chapter 2
Natural Conversations

Do you ever catch yourself talking to a bird, or a bunny rabbit, or even a tree? I do, often. It's so natural for me and it's so much fun to feel the connection—imagined or real. I've reprimanded the bunnies and squirrels, but my natural conversations have never been arguments. In fact, I've never received any kind of a response, except from my own inner voice.

My friend however, has gotten a response—from a tree! One day she was walking in the woods, feeling especially appreciative of the beauty and she impulsively walked up to a tree and gave it a hug. Being the clever punster she is, she said, "Are you lichen this?" And she immediately got a pleasant electric shock that warmed the entire length of her tall svelte body. We should all be so lucky!

I'm wondering if my grandchildren had a similar experience. Being the wise grandma I am, I took Isabel, age two and half, and Zachary, age two, for a walk around the park. With absolutely no qualms, they both did a wobbly two-year-old run up to a tree and put their arms around it when I suggested they hug the tree and thank it for its pretty leaves and its shade. They even said "thank you" in their soft round little voices. I was so alive in that tender moment, my body was relaxed and I laughed with delight as they ran back and hugged me!

It seems easy for small children to connect with nature, and yet, fears often hinder enjoyment of certain things. As a little girl, I was afraid of snakes. Until recently, I didn't know much about the snake as a symbol either, except that it was a reminder of the so-called "sinfulness" of Eve. A mystical experience with a snake a couple years ago opened my mind to seeing the symbol of the snake in a powerful, positive light. I was experiencing a very difficult transition in my life, a failed business dream, and I was very tired and fearful of the unknown. As usual, I sought to find some solace in nature. I was walking in the woods near the Mississippi River and saw the tail end of a large garter snake slither into the underbrush. The years of emotional work I had done in facing many of my fears paid off because instead of reacting like the long ago frightened little girl, I wasn't afraid; in fact, I was disappointed that I missed the chance to have a conversation with it, albeit a quick one. I stood still for a moment and then spoke out loud. I said to the snake that I hoped we would have another chance to connect because I wanted to listen to her wisdom. Thirty minutes later, on the way out of the woods, a smaller snake appeared on a different walking path. It stopped right in the middle of the path. It didn't move. Neither did I. Its body was stretched out and its head turned right at me. Intuitively I knew I was being told not to be afraid of the present or the future. To demonstrate that I was willing to face my fears, I knew I needed to touch the snake. I needed to prove that I had the courage and commitment to follow my dreams. I did it. I stroked the snake—three times. And then she slithered away. I was left standing on the path with my mouth open in surprise, my stomach in knots, and my arm tense and tingling. My mind was racing with the thoughts: How would I ever explain this? Why do I have to? Who cares? I know what happened.

It took a few minutes, but when my head and heart calmed down, I knew I had been in a two-way conversation without words, an intuitive knowing and an energetic connection with a universal wisdom.

Now, instead of symbolizing sin, the coiled up kundalini energy of the snake represents the importance of releasing emotions that keep me in pain. It reminds me that I must be grounded in wisdom in order to safely connect with the powerful feminine energy of healing that raises me to new levels of consciousness.

Many years ago, when I was the busy young mother of three little girls, my brother Mark invited me, no, he strongly encouraged me, to get up to the wilderness area in northern Minnesota. He said the views of Lake Superior were breathtaking and the forest hikes were exhilarating. I reminded him of how much I disliked "ruff'n it" and how deathly afraid I was of deep water. But I promised him I would—some day.

A couple years later, I kept that promise. And I am forever grateful for his invitation. The North Shore has now become my place of refuge. It is where I am able to stay in the present moment with greater ease. It is where I am most able to stand in awe of the power of creative energy and

I feel alive in every cell of my body when I am that connected to nature.

Like my conversation with the snake, I have conversations with Lake Superior. Watching and listening to the rolling waves crash against the rocks I hear the message of how unique we all are and yet how we are all from the same source energy. The wave *is* the lake! A unique expression of it, yet one with it. And so magnificent in its power! Just like us, especially when we face our fears.

I have found that my appreciation for life is magnified when I have consciously placed myself at risk, no matter how inconsequential the risk may seem to others. I've canoed on cold, clear, very deep forest lakes, jumped from rock to rock in a river underneath a thunderous waterfall, sat on a ledge at the top of the highest waterfall in Minnesota, hiked miles deep into national forests, and walked carefully along narrow cliffs in the red rocks of Sedona. I've also made love in the open on an island in the middle of a wilderness lake and I've sung songs for peace with amazing women under a full moon on the rocky shore of Lake Superior simply for the enjoyment and the beauty!

By facing some of my deepest fears in nature, I have strengthened my courage in facing fears in other areas of my life, like starting my own company, twice, speaking my truth at meetings, holding fast to my dreams and stepping outside my comfort zones to make them happen. I've also let go of the dreams I no longer desire, grieved the loss of loved ones, and worked courageously at discovering my authentic self.

Nature has been and continues to be a teacher of ancient wisdom and universal principles for me.

Personal connections

* Write down an unforgettable moment you experienced in nature. Don't elaborate, just jot it down. Now write down three more. Now three more. Now write down three more.

What is the common thread throughout these experiences?

*Write a brief paragraph about a moment you had in nature within the last twenty-four hours.

How is this a metaphor for your life right now?

How can these new insights deepen the love in your life?

Chapter 3
The Small Universe

Did you know that every element of the earth *and* the stars is in our body? We are truly made of stardust! The lines of my neatly organized mental box were blown away the first time I heard that this was a scientific fact and not just a poetic phrase. I was stunned and awed at the same time, and I was left with my thoughts tumbling in a space as black as night. I felt so significantly insignificant!

This new information was so exciting to me at age thirty-something that it inspired me to begin a quest to blend scientific information with my strong desire for spiritual experiences. I took a *Stars and the Universe* class at the community college with my husband not long after my interest was piqued about my body being made of stardust. It was a fascinating class and one of the highlights was seeing the film *The Power of 10*. Through the power of microscopes, we saw pictures of the universe that were indescribable in their detail and their beauty. We also saw pictures that reflected the inner universe of our bodies. As I watched, I was startled every time I realized I was looking deeper into the unseen layers of my body. It was the first time I was aware of the enormous space between the atoms in our bodies. The "no-thing-ness" within our body and its similarity with the expansiveness of the Universe was a comparison I never knew to make. Prior to seeing that film, I had never, ever thought of my body as a miniature world of open spaces and evolving systems. Seeing the complexity and the intelligence of my body from that perspective filled me with a feeling of appreciation so profound that it brought me to tears.

My capacity to grasp the details of the sciences of cosmology, physiology, and quantum physics is negligible, but I often grasp the meaning and implications very quickly and I have heard myself saying to others, "I don't understand it, but I do get it!"

Take for instance, the studies done by Masaru Emoto as described in his book *The Hidden Messages in Water* and highlighted in the movie *What the Bleep*. The idea that water crystals change when specific, concentrated thoughts are directed toward them is fascinating, and yet not explainable by me. But, I believe it. I know our bodies are made up of 70% water, and that means I get to choose my thoughts and words carefully since now I know that my body and yours are affected by words. Remember that old saying: *Sticks and stones may break my bones, but names will never hurt me*? It's not true. What we call each other and what we say to ourselves is scientifically proven to have the power to impact the physiology of our bodies.

I wasn't always aware of the intriguing mystery of my body. For most of my life I had seen it as a nuisance to take care of every morning and as a possible vehicle for pleasure. My body and I were not good friends; in fact, we were often at odds. The time it took to take care of it seemed to disrupt my life and I was often not pleased with how it performed or how it looked. I was no athletic star and I was never a beauty queen.

As a teenager, I was too tall for many boys, wore glasses, was ten to fifteen pounds too fat; my smile wasn't perfect and with my fair Irish skin, I never had a beautiful tan. I bought in to way too many of Madison Avenue's marketing campaigns, and I felt caught between the idea of my body as a temple of the Holy Spirit and a vehicle for sinful pleasure. The pleasure part was much more appealing. I still struggle at times with accepting my body with its imperfect smile, stretch marks, sagging breasts, failing eyes, wrinkles, and graying hair. But the struggle now isn't so much about the failure of my body to be what I wish for, as it is the sadness that I didn't appreciate what I had when I had it!

There is another difference in the struggle now too. A new consciousness around health began to emerge for me back in the late 1970s when I started to pursue the blending of science and spirituality. I became interested in holistic health and preventive care. I studied how what we eat affects our health, how our emotions affect our physical bodies, and how our body can heal itself using complimentary and alternative techniques, such as rolfing, acupuncture, energy healing, intuition, chiropractic, and biofeedback. I've used all of them, as well as traditional western medicine. They have all worked for me at various times under various circumstances.

Aside from a broken arm at the age of ten and delivering our three daughters, I have never been in the hospital. But I did come close a couple years ago. I was in the throes of a dark night of the soul following the failure of a business and I was menopausal. My back hurt intensely—not the usual muscle aches. I went to my holistic practitioner and she immediately said it was my liver. I said, no, it was my back. She gently insisted. I was struggling with her diagnosis, but in an emergency ultrasound several days later, her diagnosis was confirmed. I had a cyst on my liver. I knew enough about our bodies' chakra system to know that all my emotions of anger and resentment and fear had gotten stuck in my solar plexus, so I began a healing regime that integrated my physical, emotional, mental and spiritual self. My mind, body and soul became partners in healing and today I have a healthy liver because I worked at integrating all aspects of my trinity.

Now I am totally committed to the idea that my body is a miracle to be revered and taken care of. I still struggle with always choosing the healthy alternatives to food and recreation, but I feel so much better when I eat the apple instead of the cookie and when I walk instead of complaining. I rejoice in all the experiences my body has given me—both the pleasurable and the painful. I can honestly say that I am grateful for all of them. I didn't say I enjoyed all of them, but I am grateful for the lessons I have learned.

And one of the lessons I've learned is that I must first embrace the things I want to change before I have the energy and will to make the changes I want to make. When I stopped complaining about my body and began to understand and appreciate it more, I experienced a greater ease in making the changes that I wanted to make. Now I talk to my body, I tell it I'm sorry when I have been careless and injured it and I also thank it often. My body has become my own personal temple to proudly take care of and enjoy.

What my body, and yours, does without any conscious effort is amazing. I breathe and I don't have to think about it. I digest my food and I don't worry about the process and who is in control. I reach out my arms to hug my husband and it is automatic. I am able to see brilliant sunrises, hear soul-touching music and dance to its rhythms, taste my dad's fresh apples, smell the sweet fragrance of a rose, and touch the soft full cheeks of my grandchildren all without knowing how. When I just stop and take a moment to realize all this, I feel an overwhelming desire to take care of my body—like a new mother wants to nurture her baby.

At times I experience the fragility of my body and at other times, its strength, and always I feel a sense of awe and respect for its abilities and its complexity. Because of the immense gratitude I feel for my body, it is my intention to take care of my body even better than I do my home or my car, since it really is the home for my soul. And because we are made of the earth and the stars, by taking care of my body I am actually honoring the entire universe and my soul as well.

Like the universe, my body is in constant change so I continue to learn about new ways to support it. Recently, at a QiQong healing session for my newly diagnosed cataracts, Master Chungyi Lin invited me to say, "*I am in the universe. The universe is in me. The universe and I combine together.*" I did it and a soft smile formed on my face. Now every time I begin a QiQong practice, I remind myself of the truth that the universe and I are one. When I stop and allow this truth to sink deep into my being, I stand in awe of the miracle and the mystery of my very own small universe.

I invite you to choose to love your body for the miracle it is. Focus on all that is incredible and working and declare that you love it unconditionally, even with its flaws and limitations. If you do, I believe you will experience a love affair that compels you to make choices from the wise voice of your heart.

Personal connections

Your body is always speaking to you. Are you listening?

* Write a seven-line poem that begins with the words: **My body...** *Each very short line begins with the last word of the previous sentence and it takes only a minute to write the entire poem. Please refrain from judging or thinking too much. Do it quickly so that you allow your intuition to do the speaking. What insight was given to you simply by addressing your body?*

* Finish these sentences—*write for at least ten minutes on each one and/or write with your opposite hand:*

I am in awe that my body....

I am having difficulty with my body...

I am grateful to be alive because...

How can these new insights deepen the love in your life?

Aware of the Mystery of the Unconscious

We give birth to ideas,
to relationships, to works of art,
to hope, to peace, to children
and to each other.

Allow the rhythms of Nature
to whisper to you.
Feel the waxing
and the waning of the moon,
the changing of the leaves,
the brewing of a storm,
the flame of love.
Accept the emotions
these rhythms bring
and dance with them.

Enjoy the gift of laughter
and embrace the blessing of tears.
Trust your intuition
and grow in wisdom.
Feed your soul with beauty
and open your heart
to loving
and being loved.

We give birth to ideas,
to relationships, to works of art,
to hope, to peace, to children
and to each other.

Adapted from an anonymous poem

Chapter 4
Oceans of Insights

Are you comfortable in water over your head? I'm not. My husband keeps telling me it doesn't matter how deep the water is I still must swim on the top! But the fear that I can't touch bottom and propel myself to the top keeps me from enjoying the startling, brilliant beauty of the sea. And what lurks beneath the cold waters is even more terrifying for me. I do not want to die being eaten alive, or by drowning for that matter. I want to take my last breath on land in the bright sunlight.

For a long time I had a similar fear of the unconscious parts of me until I admitted I enjoyed the thrill and challenge of submerging and then surfacing with new insights into who I am and how I relate to others. I am not much of a risk-taker physically, but I am a risk-taker in the emotional, mental, and spiritual realm. There I feel confident that I have a bit of control. I can emerge from the waters whenever I choose. Well, sort of. In my recent plunge into the depths of my psyche, I was submerged for much longer than I thought I could be. As a result of doing intense transformational work through various seminars and workshops, I did, however, learn to breathe under the water of pain and confusion and I began to go with the flow more easily.

As difficult as it is at times, the search for the answer to the question of "what lesson am I to learn in this?" has resulted in healthier relationships and greater freedom for me. A perfect example of that is when I unpacked the emotional baggage that clung to me from the breakup of my business. It became very clear to me how I tend to retreat into needing the approval of others when faced with conflict, rather than standing in my own power as a confident woman. It took almost a year, but when I finally let go of needing to please everyone, I did choose another direction and I let go of unattainable expectations for both myself and others. After hard emotional work to heal the wounds, I now feel immense gratitude for the experience and for the friends I made along the way.

One issue that continued to nag at my serenity, however, was my belief system around prosperity. My thoughts of lack and limitation lurked like a shark under many of my dreams and I felt frantic to escape them. After reading a dozen books and spending a substantial amount of money on seminars, I finally broke free of the negative self-talk and uncovered one of my foundational beliefs—*spiritual people can't be rich*. You know the sayings—*A camel can get through the eye of a needle easier than a rich man can get to heaven* and *blessed are the poor*, and so on. Since my strongest desire has always been to live my life being a person involved in daily spiritual practices, being wealthy just wasn't compatible with this intention. Besides, the rich are selfish snobs and don't care about people. Or so I believed, subconsciously.

It was shortly after September 11 that I realized what this underlying belief had been doing to my life. Not only had this unhealthy belief been limiting my ability to personally experience financial freedom and serenity, it was also limiting the amount of money that I could contribute to others. September 11 made it very apparent that it was time for people whose intention is loving to have the financial resources to make huge changes in our world. Now I work daily on being a person who sees wealth as a blessing to be shared and who is committed to being generous and passionate about using my gifts in service to humanity.

One of my greatest gifts is also my greatest challenge—my human mind. The idea that our thoughts create our reality certainly isn't new, it is an ancient wisdom, and yet for me, I've only been consciously aligned with this idea for the last few years. I've heard things like "what goes around comes around" and "what you resist persists," but I never interpreted that to mean that I had any real power to co-create my life. After I experienced a transformational training on possibility thinking, I sought the answer to the questions: *How do I do that?* and *How do I become aware of what I'm creating now?* and *How do I make things happen?*

My simple studies of science and spirituality led me to a three-fold answer: meditation, affirmations, and visualization. I committed to do all three because in many ways I wanted to change the way I viewed myself, others, and the world around me and I knew this transformation needed to happen at the subconscious level. It worked. As a result of maintaining a daily practice of these three disciplines my life is bigger and brighter because I am more tolerant, more optimistic, and even more fearless in achieving my goals now.

It has not always been easy to set aside time to quiet my mind in meditation, but it has always been worth it. In this alone time I hear the still, small voice of my own wisdom and I experience a connection to an energy that is soothing and energizing. The insights that emerge are profound and life-changing. My meditation time keeps me grounded in my current reality and it also has opened me to possibilities that are totally serend!p!tous—like writing this book!

Often, I use my daily walks as a moving meditation. I begin with a conscious intention to release with each step whatever I need to release in order to create an opening for new insights or healing. It was during my walks in the darkest days of being a wife and mother that I was moved to make decisions that were terribly difficult, but life affirming.

I've found that reciting affirmations is equal in importance to meditation. You've probably heard the saying: *Change your thinking, change your life*. I realized that I couldn't make any fundamental changes in my thought patterns if I didn't go into my subconscious and transform the intelligence of my cells. Affirmations are meant to change beliefs at a cellular level and that change in perspective is a miracle!

Saying an affirmation once or twice, or even for three weeks continuously, just isn't enough to make a lasting change. I knew constant repetition was needed for the new thoughts to become the natural way to think, so I began a daily ritual of speaking the same affirmations over and over with the intention that they would imprint the new thought patterns that I wanted in my life.

I started out by reading affirmations written by someone else, then I revised those words, and eventually I wrote my own. The affirmations are constantly evolving, as I am. At the beginning, I often argued with the affirmative statement. It went something like this: "I am joyful and prosperous...yea right, look in the checkbook." My current reality glared at me and I felt dishonest in saying the affirmation. Then in the book *Feelings Buried Alive Never Die*...by Karol K. Truman, I read how it is difficult for our psyche to jump to the I AM statement before it consciously chooses that particular characteristic. So now any affirmation that I am in resistance to I say in three parts: *I choose being joyful and prosperous, I feel joyful and prosperous, I am joyful and prosperous!* I say them with complete acknowledgment of the present and then I breathe and release my fears, knowing that what I desire is manifested by my word. I say what I want to be true, and I know it is true. The essence of who I am *is* joyful and prosperous and I trust that what I desire is being created.

The two affirmations that have proved to be the most powerful in supporting my vision of who I am at my core arose from my experiences in transformational workshops. The first one is a simple statement of my essence: *I am a passionate, powerful, wise, and gentle woman.* Saying that *every* day for nearly ten years has had a dramatic effect on my life because it reminds me of who I am, even when I don't feel like it.

The other affirmation came from a coach's training workshop. It is a metaphor that I passionately chose to describe myself and how I show up in our world. And yes, I believe it to be very true that *I am a thunderous, magnificent waterfall powerfully moving people forward in their lives.* This truth is the reason I love my work as a retreat facilitator and it is the compelling force behind writing this book.

The third discipline that strengthens my power to co-create my life is visualization, and for me that is the fun part. I love to daydream and I'm good at it! My dreams are in vivid color and I use all my senses to create the feeling that I am actually experiencing the event. I know it's not a waste of time because it's the combination of visualizing, affirming, and feeling that causes things to happen. For ten years, I said that I was the spiritual director and owner of a retreat estate in my daily affirmations. I pictured myself welcoming visitors and presenters, and meeting with staff. I felt serene as I pictured myself walking the hiking paths and I felt the physical sensations of enthusiasm in my whole body as I saw myself embracing people after their experiences and shedding tears of joy with them. Most importantly, I worked very hard emotionally to clear away the layers of old beliefs that kept me thinking this dream was not possible. And then it happened. All the key people came together in a serend!p!tous manner and The Serend!p!ty Retreat House was manifested. My life has changed dramatically as a result of that visualized dream becoming a reality, but I continue to meditate, affirm, and visualize my life the way I intend it to be. And I am grateful beyond measure.

For many years, I have been asking the questions that take me beyond my conscious knowing. I am paying more attention to my dreams, listening to my inner voice, challenging my own beliefs, facing my shadow and embracing my shortcomings and my goodness. I know diving into the mystery of the unconscious is both freeing and frightening and for me; that is the adventure part of living a full life. I also know the insights that emerge expand the love and joy in my life and that reward is priceless.

The deep sea (figuratively and literally) is a place of healing and beauty, as well as terror. I didn't think I would ever have the courage to snorkel in the azure waters of the Caribbean, but now that I have been in the dark waters of my psyche and emerged into the bright sunlight, I am committed to experiencing the thrill of seeing the exquisite life forms beneath the surface of the sea. I want to see the myriad of brilliant colors and I want to feel a sense of oneness with the ocean. Besides, I want to conquer my fear. And I will.

Personal connections
* Choose an object, anything that you are drawn to and can physically see at this moment.
Journal about this object.
How is this a metaphor for your life right now?

* In the ocean of your psyche, what issues are you most afraid to face?
How would your life be different if you released the fear?
What new way of being would you choose?

* Write an affirmation that expresses your essence. Share it with someone you trust.
Affirm it every day.

How can these new insights deepen the love in your life?

Chapter 5
Gifts from Mother

What issue have you been struggling with all your life? Have you found the core question from which it arises? I believe I discovered mine after fifty years of being in the dark.

I was conceived in love and born in shame. In 1949 it was a disgrace for a couple to have a baby just two months after their marriage. But that is my beginning. And it took almost half a century for both my mother and myself to heal the wound of that unplanned pregnancy. My challenge was to accept that I had a right to be here and her challenge was to embrace her worthiness.

I received the letter from my parents telling me my birthday was only two months after their marriage, *rather than fourteen months*, when I was eighteen years old. I was away at college and I was in a serious relationship with my boyfriend/husband-to-be. I think they wanted to warn me. I was stunned at the information and I cried for two days. I felt betrayed by the hidden secret and a bit embarrassed, but not mortified. I also felt a sense of relief because now my own sexuality seemed much less intimidating and my sexual activity more acceptable.

I said I cried for two days, and really that's about all. It just wasn't a tragedy to me. I thought of the act of lovemaking as a gift and a baby as a miracle. And I was more involved with creating my own new adult life than thinking about my parents' young adult life. We never talked about it either, so I thought all was well and good. Except there was this low-grade tension between Mom and me and I struggled to figure out the real issues between us. Then in my fiftieth year, I attended yet another human potential seminar and I participated in an exercise where I wrote out my life story and then read it aloud. I spoke it again and again and again…dozens of time, until I was sick of hearing my story and the obvious finally broke free from my subconscious. *Did they want me? Did they want to adopt me out to another couple? Should I have been born? Did I have a right to be here?*

I wanted a celebration for my fiftieth birthday and I wanted them to celebrate their fiftieth anniversary so I invited them to have a conversation about the secret. They accepted the invitation. It happened in my home around my grandma's beautiful oak dining table with the sun shining through glass doors and the candle on the table glowing softly. I shared my fear they might have wanted to give me away. Mom cried softly. Dad shared. He said they never considered giving me away, but they did consider running away. I cried. Dad cried. We all cried softly from feelings of relief and feelings of love as deep as the ocean.

A gala Fiftieth Anniversary party for my parents was the healing salve that brought me closure to this event that had gone unspoken for many years. And it brought great peace to my soul.

I stand in great admiration for my mother and I enjoy her Irish laughter and her willingness to "do a lot of things for the people I love." She has been my role model of courage and commitment and spiritual seeker. I honor the qualities I inherited from her. Those aspects I don't like, I work on healing in myself.

My own experience of motherhood followed in the footsteps of my mom: our first daughter was born only six months after our wedding. However, this time there was a celebration. And Mom and Dad supported it. It had been my childhood yearning to be married and to become a mom and besides, I enjoyed the sex. My dreams had come true and I felt ecstatic, so why not a party! What a difference between 1949 and 1969. I had a large church wedding, got married in white, and we had a fun reception.

Our first daughter was born and we rejoiced. Our second daughter was born and we rejoiced. Our third daughter was born and we rejoiced. We also said, "We're done." The physical births were complete, but the learning had just begun. And I was the student.

My daughters were and still are my greatest teachers. Everything I thought I knew and believed has been challenged at the very core belief. I mean everything. My values involving life and love, as well as my personality traits and behaviors, have been placed under their microscope and my own in order to more fully understand our relationships. I've learned that there is always more than one way to look at things and my way isn't always the right way. Their lessons helped me evolve from being a rigid "either/or" person to being someone who works at finding the "both/and" in situations and events.

One situation taught me this truth: motherhood and marriage aren't always partners. That became crystal clear with the first of three pregnancies of our two unwed daughters. As much as my husband and I valued the experience of marriage, we knew our two daughters were not ready for it and we chose to support them in raising their daughters as single moms. For us, it was the right thing to do and even with all the tumultuous feelings of guilt and embarrassment, we have absolutely no regrets. I often whisper in the ears of those three unexpected granddaughters, "I'm sooooooo glad you were born."

My daughters have much to tell about their experiences as mothers and daughters. Someday they will write their own books about how they healed the relationship with their mom, and for each one of them the story will focus on a different shortcoming of mine. What I know for sure is that we were meant to be in this relationship simply because we are. They have taught me lessons on loving unconditionally and I know I have taught them lessons of courage through both my wisdom and my fear.

We are all sons and daughters of a mother, and inherent in that role is the soul-learning our mothers have to teach us. Learning to accept nurturing and learning to be the nurturer is one of the lessons. For many of us, that lesson was not learned from our birth mother. It might have been learned from a teacher, a relative, or a sibling. It might even have been learned from a man or maybe from a beloved pet. Whoever the messenger, the message is this…"You are lovable, you are loved, and you are loving."

Giving birth to children is certainly a gift, but it is not the only way to learn life's lessons or to be creative. We have all created something, be it a book, a garden, a painting, a clean home, a poem, a new way of being, a relationship, a new hot dish, a business deal, whatever. I've never created a masterpiece for a museum, and yet, I know I'm very creative. I have designed experiences that have transformed the way people look at things. And more importantly, I've redesigned myself into a person that can turn the ordinary into the extraordinary simply by seeing things from more than one perspective.

Man or woman, we are all pregnant with something right now too. If we are alive, we are growing something within our psyche, and it is to our advantage to become conscious of what that is. Mythology is full of stories of the gods eating their children because of their ego fears. Being aware of what our thoughts are producing is the first step in making choices that create more love and joy in our lives.

The second step to creating more love and joy in our lives is to be grateful. For everything—blessings *and* struggles. It seems like it would be easy to always say "thank you" for gifts given and everyday blessings, but that isn't true. Too often I've found myself taking them for granted and when I realize it, a heartfelt word of appreciation spoken aloud can make the difference between serenity and anxiety. Taking the time to actually say the words "thank you" makes my body feel lighter for a moment, my mind freer of confusion, and my soul joyful!

When I'm feeling sorry for myself, if I stop and choose to see the lesson in the pain and give thanks for the learning, I immediately feel better. Even the unappreciated lessons of life are worth looking at from a new perspective. If we choose, they are always a blessing and we can be sincerely grateful.

I love this quote from the beautiful children's book *The Secret of Saying Thanks* by Douglas Wood, "We don't give thanks because we're happy. We are happy because we give thanks." I can only imagine my life if I would remain conscious to that simple wisdom all the time.

Personal connections

*Take ten minutes and list all the names of mother figures in your life. *Who nurtured you and by doing so, taught you how to nurture others?*
List twelve gifts or qualities you received from them.

*Journal about these questions: *What are you pregnant with right now? What stage of the pregnancy are you in? Are you about to deliver or are you still unsure of the outcome and feeling sick? What are the feelings you have around this expected birth? How will this newborn affect your life? What will you do to make sure that giving birth is healthy and safe for you? Or should this pregnancy be aborted? How does saying you are pregnant with this project affect your feelings about it?*

How will these new insights deepen the love in your life?

Chapter 6
Underneath It All

Have you taken any personality profile tests? Yes? Which one offered you the greatest clarity in identifying your attributes? Isn't it amazing how accurate they are?

I've taken several tests and all have been very helpful in my process of self-discovery. I've also read many books on self-help psychology and attended numerous seminars and they have been invaluable as well. Feeding my mind with new information makes me full of questions that help me peel off the layers of old beliefs that keep me from knowing the truth of who I am.

Through all this psychological exploring, I found the concept of archetypes to be the most helpful. According to Dr. Edward Edinger, "An archetype is to the psyche what an instinct is to the body." A simple explanation is that they are the universal thought patterns, the primordial energies that underlie human consciousness. Dr. Carl Jung, famous psychologist of the last century, was instrumental in identifying the archetypes of our collective unconscious. He clearly showed us how each of us is uniquely ourselves while still being part of a collective whole. Questions like: *Who am I? Why am I here? Do I really get to choose?* are all universal questions. The answers however, are very specific to each individual. It excites me to know that I am a unique individual, as well as a member of an evolving human species on a common journey.

In the course of my work to be aware of the mystery of my unconscious, I uncovered my seven strongest archetypal thought patterns. Six of them are obvious to me and anyone who knows me. One of them was a surprise!

I am a leader—no surprise on that one! This is the thought pattern that has influenced my entire life and it has been both a gift and a challenge. Balancing my tendencies to be opinionated and controlling with my natural empathy for others and my ability to take creative action is often an internal struggle, but the clearer I am about who I am, the easier the balance seems to happen. It also gets easier to choose in what areas I will use my energy to be the leader. I no longer have to be in charge of everything!

I know that as a leader, I stir things up and oftentimes even "rock the boat." For myself, and many others, this is uncomfortable, but I know I embody this warrior archetype, and I know it is necessary. Often times, I reluctantly say "yes" to the inner call to challenge a system or an individual, but when I consciously act as a loving leader with the courage of the warrior I feel satisfied that I have been authentic in the relationship.

Being a leader and warrior puts me out on the edge and in that position I can fall into playing the role of victim or martyr. To break this archetypal thought pattern, I am constantly asking myself the questions: *What is the payoff in continuing to think this way? Is it worth the price I'm paying? What would my life be like if I released these thoughts and the feeling of being a victim and instead, chose to stand in my own power?* When I answer these questions honestly, I teach myself new ways of being.

It seems like I've been teaching forever too, so this archetype is not a surprise either. I've taught siblings how to tie shoes, daughters how to experience life safely, and adults how to be leaders, and no matter what it is I teach, I realize now that I always learn more than I teach. Several years ago I read the book *The Four-Fold Way* by Angeles Arrien and the insights I gleaned were profound. Arrien's suggestion that a teacher use the three tools of *silence, ancestor spirits* and *meditation* resonated within me. And her idea that dance is a healing salve for teachers was right on for me because it is something I thoroughly enjoy doing!

When I first heard the story of Don Quixote as a young girl, I had very mixed feelings. I yearned to have people believe in him and his dreams, but I also felt frustrated and thought "get realistic." That sums up a big part of my life. I have dreams yet unfulfilled that are a direct result of my impossible dreamer archetype. Reminding myself that this archetype is a major component of my psyche helps me be courageous enough to act on my dreams and persevere until they are realized. As the teacher, I know I get to let go of the outcome, but as the dreamer, I get to visualize the desired goal. This creative tension motivates me and keeps me enthusiastic.

The archetype of godseeker is the driving force behind all the others. From the time I was a little girl, I knew I wanted to get to know God. I had a million questions and several numinous experiences that increased my longing to have an intimate relationship with this mysterious power. Intellectually learning more about the immanent and transcendent nature of God has enhanced my understanding of God, but my personal experiences as a parent, lover, and friend have led me to my core beliefs about God.

Now here's the surprise: the *goddess* archetype is a huge thought pattern in my life. When I did the work suggested by Carolyn Myss in her book *Sacred Contracts*, I was amazed at how much of my life was influenced by the goddess archetype. And the irony of it is that I hated the study of mythology in freshman English class. I thought the stories of the Greek gods and goddesses were ridiculous and totally irrelevant to my life. Shows how little a fourteen-year-old knows!

Actually, I've learned the goddess archetypes are sacred stories that help us understand the mystery of our lives. They are the ancient energies inherent in each of us and these energies are most easily understood in the form of myths. According to Dr. Robert Johnson, author of the books *She*, *He*, and *We*, "myths are a special kind of literature not written or created by a single individual, but produced by the imagination and experience of an entire age and culture and they can be seen as the distillation of the dreams and experiences of a whole culture…Myths, therefore, portray a collective image, they tell us about things that are true for all people." Simply put, myths are stories that speak a profound truth and help us understand our humanness. They give meaning to our lives and help us see beyond our personal limitations to a greater mystery. Myths can help us discover and access our awesome innate power. The goddess myths are stories of women and their relationships with men, other women, and their children. They are our stories.

Goddesses in Everywoman by Jean Shinoda Bolen was a life-changing book for me. It included the stories of the seven major goddess archetypes of ancient Greece and Rome. Their stories presented the complexities of being a woman and helped me see more clearly my own uniqueness. It also opened my eyes to the distinct archetypal energies of my daughters, my granddaughters, and all the other women in my life. Now it is much easier to understand these relationships because knowing their basic archetype allows me to more quickly release any judgments and it helps me see and appreciate their qualities. As a result of reading the book, I now appreciate mythology as an imaginative visual aid for diving deep into my subconscious and for understanding the universality of our human joys and struggles.

When I first reflected on the meaning and implications of the goddess archetype in my life, I found myself in resistance to the whole idea. That immediately told me I needed to bring the idea into the light of consciousness because I have found that anything I resist needs to be healed in some way. So I decided to fearlessly answer the questions: *What is a goddess? Am I a goddess? How is being a goddess relevant for a woman today? How does being a goddess affect my belief in a spiritual being?*

In the next few pages, I will share with you my personal insights on those questions, and my understanding of God. As you read, I invite you to reflect on what my explanations mean to you and how they relate to your life. Challenge my beliefs and your own.

For me, the concept of goddess does not define a supreme being to be worshipped; instead, a goddess is a personification of the attributes and shortcomings of our humanness. Every culture has its stories and various names for the goddess energies, and every person, man or woman, has the goddess energies within them. The energies of commitment, independence, destruction, and creativity, are only a few of the many energies inherent in the different goddess archetypes and inherent within each of us.

I found it easy to relate to the stories of the goddesses, but I was very reluctant to call myself a goddess. It was one thing to acknowledge a divine feminine energy within me, but to call it goddess seemed blasphemous or at the very least, arrogant. The ancient wisdom traditions invite us to know and embrace the feminine, nurturing nature of God, so I wondered what made it hard for me to call myself a goddess.

After much reflection, I decided I was struggling with the idea that I could be divine even with all my imperfections. My perception of the divine feminine was one of gentleness, passivity, nurturing and *perfect* womanhood. Whatever that was, it sure wasn't me. Often I am assertive, loud, opinionated and feel too fat—certainly not a "perfect" woman. I professed that my essence was whole, complete, and perfect, but in fact, my self-proclaimed imperfections were what I often identified with. So how was I to reconcile these two seemingly opposing ideas? How could I be a goddess and imperfect at the same time?

After attending a class on Jung psychology and studying more about the archetypes, I decided that being a goddess today simply means experiencing the whole of who I am—physically, mentally, emotionally and spiritually. And with that definition, I claimed the title. I began a journey I was surprised to be taking in the name of being a goddess. I re-committed to exploring the unknown parts of me and to celebrating the parts I do know in order to embrace the fullness of who I am. As a goddess today, I get to rejoice in both my feminine qualities and my masculine qualities and when I do, I stand in the power of my authentic self to nurture ideas and to do what is needed to manifest my dreams. That is being a co-creator of my life.

Underneath it all, my resistance to accepting myself as a goddess stemmed from the fear of embracing my own divinity. I believe that I am a spiritual being having a human experience, but my ego fears of being rejected and ridiculed often kept me from embracing this truth of who I am. Writing my own personal goddess declaration was the breakthrough moment for me that caused me to move through the fear. I was desperate to free myself from hurt feelings and to stand as a woman of wisdom. It worked. I now proudly call myself a goddess and lead women in circles where they discover their own goddess beauty. For me, the answer to the question "Am I a goddess?" is now a reverberating "YES!"

My experience is that once I claimed the title and embraced the significance of being a goddess, I was then able to let go of the label. I now freely choose to identify with the concept of goddess whenever it serves to enhance my acceptance of my authentic self, but I no longer need it to claim my divinity.

What I know to be true is that when I stay aware of the mystery of the unconscious serend!p!tous discoveries occur or old ideas are made new and more questions are created for me to explore.

Personal connections:
* Make a list of what you consider to be feminine qualities. Make a list of what you consider to be masculine qualities.
Does your image of God include the qualities on both your lists?

How does the idea of being a goddess fit into your beliefs about God?

* If you feel moved to do so, read the goddess declaration on the following page aloud—three times.

What emotions are evoked in you? Journal about the words that speak to your heart.

How will these new insights deepen the love in your life?

Goddess Declaration

I freely and wholeheartedly choose to accept my role
as a goddess whose life shines a light of
Truth, Honor, Love and Joy into our world.
I will do this by...

Honoring my divinity,
So that I am able to honor yours.

Accepting the truth of my shortcomings with dignity,
So that I am able to accept yours.

Accepting the truth of my strengths with pride & joy,
So that I am able to accept yours.

Rejoicing in my human physical needs and desires,
So that I am able to rejoice in yours.

Nurturing myself with gentleness,
So that I am gentle with you.

Valuing my thoughts,
So that I value yours.

Respecting my wisdom,
So that I respect yours.

Trusting my intuition,
So that I trust yours.

Celebrating my creativity,
So that I celebrate yours.

ALIVE, AWARE, AWAKE

Recognizing my own beauty,
So that I may see how beautiful you are.

I will do this by…

Opening my heart to feeling worthy,
So that I experience your worthiness.

Accepting your love,
So that I can love others.

I will accept my role as a goddess by imagining a world of peace, where all people are conscious of their oneness with Spirit and with each other,

Beginning here, beginning now
From this moment to forever…..*I am a goddess!*

Awake to the Mystery of Spirit

Without the God there is no Goddess.
Without the Goddess there is no God.
How sweet is their love!

Chapter 7
The Awe in God

Have you ever wondered what the distinction is between soul and spirit? It seems so many of us use the two words interchangeably in relation to the concept of God. I don't think they really are interchangeable though. For me, Spirit is the energy from which everything is manifested and my soul is the unique expression of that energy. Spirit is bigger than soul and it is the source and oneness of all souls. Spirit is what I'm awake to when I'm alive and aware.

Before you go any farther into this chapter, I invite you to create a sacred space for yourself. Relax and breathe deeply. Be still for a moment. Feel yourself softening in your chair. In the stillness, set your intention to receive the following words with an open heart and open mind. I wrote them with the intention that you experience an insight that will be healing for you and bring you joy. This is a holy moment for both of us.

My relationship with God is filled with life's joys and struggles. Many of them I have already shared. The experiences I share in this chapter are the ones that most dramatically affected the evolution of my understanding of God.

The notion that four words: *to, for, through, as*, describe our intellectual and emotional process in relationship to God is not new, but I only linked them to my journey just a few years ago. Now they frame my understanding of God and they help me appreciate the mystery of spirit.

For most of my life when bad things happened it was explained away as God's will. My childhood conditioning emphasized that God does things *to* you—he punishes, he rewards, he forgives, he loves. I really didn't question this belief until October 1971.

At that time we were living in Germany because my husband, Mike, had been drafted into the Army. We had already said our prayers of thanksgiving *to* God for sending us there, instead of him being sent to

Vietnam. His tour in Germany was up in December and we were hoping to be home before Christmas.

On Friday evening, October 9, Mike came home from the base with several letters from home. I read my letter in stunned silence, and then I sobbed. My Irish twin sister, Kathy, had been diagnosed with leukemia. She was twenty-one, I was twenty-two, just eleven months older than her. I was the oldest of twelve children, she was the second oldest.

I immediately began planning how fast I could make it home. I intended to call home as soon as I knew the flight times and I planned to make those arrangements on Monday since nothing was open over the weekend. But on Sunday night, we received a call from the States. We had no phone, so we were called to our neighbors on the third floor of the building. Dad said that Kathy had developed serious complications and was not expected to live through the night. He asked me to be strong. I said I would. I hung up the phone and collapsed on the floor in tears. Kathy died nineteen days after her diagnosis and I was unable to get home before she died. She did not hear me tell her how much I loved her and that broke my heart.

The trip to get home was a nightmare and the homecoming was agonizing. All the talk that this was "God's will" by many of the relatives was not at all comforting. That answer did not satisfy me. I didn't think the reason for her death was either that simple or that cruel. I remember asking the question "Why?" over and over. It wasn't until one of my aunts, a nurse, answered it humbly by saying, "We don't know why" that I began to let go of the question, if only for the moment. She said maybe Kathy ate too many bananas, which was her way of saying there is no answer to that question.

As glib as the answer about the bananas seems, it caused a moment of awakening in me. Another possibility had been presented. I still didn't have an answer, instead I had more questions, but I felt relief that I might not have to blame God anymore.

Kathy's life was one of enthusiasm for the new, love for the questions, and strength to be daring. Our love-hate relationship was typical of sisters, but she was my best friend and giggle mate. Her unexpected death jolted me into personal introspection and questioning, and her life taught me to enjoy the moment and speak the love you have in your heart.

Remember my brother Mark? He is the one who invited me to go up to the wilderness area of Northern Minnesota. Six years after Kathy died, Mark drowned up there. He was twenty-six and I was twenty-eight.

The knock on the door in the middle of the night went unanswered by me because I looked at the face of my aunt through the window and I knew something terrible had happened. My husband had to open the door and grab me to keep me from running down the hall. My knees buckled and I collapsed when the words were spoken, ever so softly.

The very long dark night of informing siblings and waiting for the confirmation from local authorities was horrendous. When I finally came home in the morning, I was near hysterical with grief. I crawled up the stairs into our living room and Mike met me at the top. He held me as we sat there on the floor and we both sobbed. Then the phone rang. I knew it would be for me, so I answered it. It was Mike's sister and she was crying. She asked me, "How could God do this to your family again?"

I remember saying very calmly, "God didn't do this, God is crying for us." The minute I said it, I knew it was true. Years of study and struggling with the questions of God's will had paid off. I had internalized a new set of beliefs. It was another moment of awakening. God didn't do this *to* us—there was no one to blame.

Mark was number three in birth order and he was also my playmate and ally. I was devastated by his death. I felt physically cold for many months after his body was recovered from the frigid waters of the Canyon River, but the questions I asked and the lessons I learned from those questions changed the course of my life, not the least of which was the struggle over God's will. I often found myself telling people, "No, it wasn't God's will, Mark chose not to wear his life jacket and that is the adventurer he was." Mark's life was an invitation for me to go into the unknown in both natural surroundings, and in my consciousness, and I have accepted that invitation over and over. His death helped me come to an understanding of a loving, rather than a vindictive God, and that was a crucial step in my journey to the beliefs I have today.

I was brought to my knees by yet another death. Exactly twenty years after Mark died, our infant granddaughter died shortly after her birth.

Our oldest daughter married a man who lovingly embraced her other two daughters as his own and then they had a daughter. They named her Rachael Renee. Born beautiful and seemingly healthy, we were all shocked twelve hours after her birth to learn that her intestines were all twisted and that she would not survive. Her parents cuddled her and I sang the Irish lullaby to her, and fifty-four hours after she was born she died in her mother's arms. The pain of this loss was excruciating. I witnessed my daughter experiencing my worst fear and I felt helpless to take away her pain.

Feeling powerless to do anything, we could only become a loving support for one another. During this entire experience of surrender and grief the light of love shone very brightly for our family and friends.

This time there were absolutely no questions from me about why God did this to us. My understanding of God no longer held that thought. Instead, the questions were, "What did I believe about healing?" "What lessons did Rachael come to teach us?" and "What blessings did her life bring into our lives?"

Her whole brilliant little life was a blessing and one of the greatest lessons it taught me was not to take what I love for granted. Like I said to her little brother, born only a year later, "She taught us that we are loved not because of what we do, but just because we are!"

I seem to handle the really big issues in my life without blaming God anymore, but the "God does it *to* me" notion pops up unexpectedly in everyday things, such as unexpected financial burdens. Honestly, it's the mundane things that most often frustrate me and I fall into my victim archetype. I want to blame something or someone for the misfortune. It feels comfortable playing the victim, but I know it is not freeing. What I know to be true is: God is not responsible.

My relationship with God has also been one of "what can God do *for* me?" When was the last time you prayed *to* a God *for* something? At times, I still fall back into old belief patterns and I call on God, like a Santa Claus, asking for things or for events to turn out the way I want.

A recent example of that was on a trip my husband and I took driving home from Arizona to Minnesota. I need to preface this example by letting you know I am terrified of driving narrow, winding mountain roads. I am in awe of the scenery, but I sit stoned face, quiet, white knuckled, and breathing short gasps until we finally arrive at either the top or the bottom. I have lots of theories on why I am so afraid, but none of them have really helped alleviate my fears, so I pray instead.

And believe me, I prayed for safety on the road between Prescott and Sedona and on "up the hill" to Flagstaff during that March snowstorm. Obviously, God "answered my prayers" because I am writing this book. My wish is to relax and enjoy the scenery so Mike can relax and enjoy the scenery. I'm a little better than I was when we drove in the Bavarian Alps many years ago, but the struggle to let go of the fear and instead trust that I am safe, is still a huge one.

When I do get an "answered prayer" in my favor, I am very quick to say "thank you." In fact, I find it is an automatic response to thank God *for* blessings in my life. When I do that, I am not blaming God, rather, I'm giving God credit.

It seems to me, however, that when I'm relating to God in these two ways, *to* and *for*, I am living from an Old Testament type mentality. Something many of us do—it's our childhood conditioning. We think we are separate from God—he is out there and we need to stay connected to him.

The next two words—*through* and *as*—describe how I relate to God from the higher consciousness of the New Testament.

Do you know the Prayer of St. Francis? I learned it as a child and said it off and on, mostly through a song that was sung at church. But many years ago, I began to move my consciousness to a new level of awareness when I chose to say the prayer regularly and with clear intention.

Lord, make me an instrument of thy peace,
Where there is hatred, let me sow love,
Where there is injury, pardon,
Where there is doubt, faith,
Where there is despair, hope,
Where there is darkness, light, and
Where there is sadness, joy.

Oh Divine Master, grant that I may not so much seek to be consoled, as to console. To be understood, as to understand, to be loved, as to love. For it's in giving that we receive, it's in pardoning, that we are pardoned, and it's in dying that we are born to eternal life.

I think a clear metaphor for this type of relationship with God is the electric transformer. When I think of God as the power or the electricity, then I see myself as the transformer or the light bulb.

There are many blessings relating to God that way, both personally, and for the world. Often I pray to be a positive channel for love, or healing, or wisdom. I sincerely want to use my life to make a loving difference in the lives of others and I can't even imagine a world where people aren't working for peace, or taking care of the sick, or teaching our children, or feeding the hungry. St. Francis calls all of us to use our gifts in service to others. However, a relationship where the power is outside of us still keeps us in a relationship where we are separate from God. We are doing the work *for* God.

Life is full of paradox. The older I get the easier it is for me to accept that life does not consist of ideas or situations that are simply either/or. Have you ever said to yourself, "Well, I'm only human!" and accepted it as the truth. Have you ever heard someone else say it and thought, "Well, that's an excuse!"

The fourth word used to understand an evolving relationship with God is *as*. This word describes the highest level of consciousness in relating to God. In fact, the highest level is not about relating *to* God at all, but rather it is about *being an individual expression of a spiritual energy.*

Reading the book *The Universe Is Calling* by Eric Butterworth had a profound impact on my life. It helped me understand more of the mystery of God. At least it helped me articulate the questions I had been asking all my life. Rev. Butterworth writes:

God is not in you in the same sense that a raisin is in a bun. That is not unity. God is in you as the ocean is in the wave. The wave is nothing more nor less than the ocean expressing as a wave.

This metaphor of the ocean and wave is huge for me. It helps me grasp the idea that we are all one. We are not the whole of the ocean, but we are the ocean expressed in a single wave. We are not the transformer or the light bulb, we are actually the electricity, manifesting as lightening or the electricity powering the light bulb! Wow! Think of it. We are truly that powerful—we *can* do what Jesus says: "*All these things you can do, and even more!*"

Rev. Butterworth makes another very profound distinction. He says, "God is Love, rather than God is loving." Think about that for a moment. What is the distinction for you? He makes it very clear that God is not a benevolent man or woman to whom we should pray. That anthropomorphic image is a left-over belief from our Old Testament mentality. My own journey in relationship to the mystery of God has also resulted in the shedding of an anthropomorphic being. In fact, I now find it difficult to even embrace the notion that I am a child of God. Being a "child" evokes in me a sense of separation, even rebelliousness, and too often that makes for a disconnected relationship.

Instead, I believe God is the pure vibrational energy that creates. And that is an idea that fits with all the new science of today. Science has shown that love is the highest vibrational energy and it is everywhere present—all the time. Isn't that our definition of God? If we are the wave in an ocean of love then at our very core we are love. This truth is a beautiful blend of science and spirituality. Human beings are expressing *AS* the Universal Life Force Energy of Love. We are mysterious, we are magnificent, and we are holy.

People have been in awe of this Mystery since the beginning of time. We have given it names such as God, Yahweh, Allah, and Buddha and now the world is birthing new names to describe it. These names are inclusive and bigger than a human image. They express the intimate, creative relationship of lovers and parents and artists. They capture the fullness of being human and the awe of the divine. Some call the great mystery Sacred Spirit. Some call it Goddessence. Others call it the Universe or Source or Higher Self. The name I've given it is G*AW*ED.

This unique spelling combines my sense of awe in the power of creation with the universal sound expressed by many when speaking of the Mystery. This is the surround sound of the universe! Just listen! Do you hear the awe in your life? Can you see it? Do you feel it? Are you open to *being* the awe in our world? Are you ready to acknowledge and embrace the awesome energy within you?

From deep within my heart, I intuitively know this to be true: We are human, *and* we are divine. The very essence of us is divine, it is our core. When we dissolve all our fears, what we are left with is divine love—the substance of our being! The magnificent truth that my soul is unique, and our souls are one in the Mystery of Spirit is the energy that brings the sacred into my ordinary life and it is that same energy that keeps me feeling alive, aware, and awake!

A Meditation

Embracing Your Divinity

Continue to be in this quiet, relaxed place
Breathe deeply
Begin at your toes ~ relax
Feel your feet grounded to the earth
Breathe in confidence
Exhale and allow your breath to gently blow away fear
Breathe in serenity
Exhale and allow your breath to gently blow away frustrations
Breathe in acceptance
Exhale and allow your breath to gently blow away confusion
Move your breath up your entire body ~ slowly
Breathe
Feel Love flowing throughout your entire body
Relax

Place your hand on your heart
Breathe a breath of LOVE to your heart
See the glimmer of light deep within your heart
Breathe LOVE to that light
Watch that light grow and encompass your heart
Feel the light encompass your heart
Feel the light grow brighter and more brilliant
Feel the light permeate your entire body
Feel the light warm you with gentleness
This is the Divine in you
This LIGHT is the essence of YOU
This Light is LOVE manifested as you
You are LOVE loving!
Be with this…

ALIVE, AWARE, AWAKE

Know this is Truth…
You are LOVE loving
You are a Sacred Expression of Spirit
You are Spirit expressing as you
You are the Essence.
You are LIGHT and LOVE
Feel the AWE in knowing this.
Feel the Power in knowing this…
You do make a difference.
You are changing the world being your authentic self.
Feel the excitement in knowing you are meant to be on earth.
Feel Love and Acceptance for who you are.
Embrace this Truth
You are Spirit expressing as you.
Feel the joy knowing this, and smile.

A Heroine's Journey

The chief of the Artemis tribe chose a virgin from the Persephone tribe. Their first born, a daughter, was conceived in lustful love and born in shame before the celebration ritual. She was named Vendia. When she was only a very small girl, Vendia was carried away by a grieving brown bear. She was taught the ways of the forest by the she-bear. She adapted to the long, quiet winters and learned to trust all the forest animals, except the snake, which always seemed to sneak up on her. She grew strong and independent and returned to her tribe to find a suitable mate. She chose a strong warrior from the Athena tribe and they bore three daughters. Because of her keen senses she became the trusted sentry and protector warrior of the Artemis tribe. Eventually, Vendia became the chief and the tribe wanted more fertile land. She went exploring and discovered a lake deep in the forest. She was very thirsty. The forest animals whispered not to go near the lake because drinking from it would cause her to forget who she was, the snake said it would quench her thirst. Her thirst overpowered her and she decided to take the risk. She got sucked into the depths of the lake. She spiraled down, down, down. At lake bottom there was a narrow hole and in a suffocating tight squeeze she was propelled through. VenDia hit bottom with a painful jolt and noticed she was surrounded by rabbits, all different kinds and billions of them. Some were thumping her, others nibbling on her body, others fighting with each other—all very annoying. She heard the voice of her friend, the forest wolf, tell her to embrace the bunny. As soon as she picked one up and cuddled it, they all disappeared. But in their place, appeared trillions of flying bats, all swooping down on her and trying to drag her off. Their high-pitched scream and their evil faces gave no mercy. Then she heard the voice of her trusted friend, the she bear. She commanded Vendia to take off her clothes and stand naked. She listened and reluctantly obeyed and the bats left, carrying away her clothes. But now she was standing naked with gazillions of buzzing mosquitoes swarming around her and biting and biting and biting—again and again. Then she heard the silent slither of the big snake. The snake hissed at her and began to approach her. She froze. Then she watched as the snake began to encircle her. The tongue whipped in large circular motions, swallowing all the mosquitoes. It continued to encircle her body, tightly wrapping itself around her as it continued to eat up all the nasty insects. When she was completely enveloped by it, the snake began to slither up through the long dark hole.

When they reached the water, it glided to the surface and then submerged again. It did this again. And again. The fourth time, it emerged from the water and crawled onto dry land. It unwrapped itself from Vendia and lay coiled up next to her. She stroked it– three times in gratitude. Vendia went back to the tribe to teach them what she had learned and then she led them through the bountiful forest and to the thirst-quenching lake.

Personal Connections

Just for fun you might want to write your story in the form of a myth. I did this for a Jung class and I was amazed at how much I enjoyed using my imagination and how provocative the images are. Seeing my life from this symbolic viewpoint was very helpful in embracing my life story.

In my myth, the rabbits represent all the births that have occurred in my life, the bats represent all the deaths, and the mosquitoes all the money issues.

What symbols would you use to describe your life events?

Afterword

I am the oldest of seven sisters. I have three daughters, five granddaughters, and fourteen nieces. I went to an all-girls high school and college and I lead women's workshops and retreats. I am so full of gratitude for these blessings that often I feel like a cup over flowing.

I didn't always enjoy being with women, however. In fact, I was sick to death of them by the time I quit college. I hated the cattiness and the competition. I was much more comfortable with men. But my ego hates feeling left out, so when I was invited to join a women's spiritual support group in 1974, I did, and my life was transformed. It was a watershed moment on my spiritual journey. What I discovered in the support group was a wealth of wisdom and camaraderie that was sorely needed in my life. I gasped at the beauty I saw in the vulnerability and authenticity of the women on a similar path. And I began to stand in awe of who we are and who we can be. It opened me to seeing things in new ways, to trusting with less fear, and to moving beyond my old experiences and beliefs. It was in this group that I met my dearest friend and our souls have been touching for over thirty years.

Being a part of that support group helped me realize I need to tell my story and it's my belief we all do. That doesn't mean repeatedly complaining or replaying the victim role over and over. Rather, it is about focusing on the lesson learned so that we are able to let go of the emotional charge of the past experience and open up our mind and heart to enjoy the present moment. Telling our stories to illuminate the deeper truth and eliminate blame opens space for forgiveness. It also allows us to see the experiences from a new perspective and that can be a healing miracle.

I know I am a woman of wisdom and I believe you are too. We each have within us a wellspring of knowledge and experience that connects us to one another in ways that are mysterious and illuminating. When I listen to women's stories as either a friend or facilitator, I am offered the gifts of tenderness and strength, of brokenness and wholeness, of surrender and power, and of tears and laughter. I know that by using the power of our stories we can change our lives and in so doing we change our world.

I take seriously the invitation for women to be the change we want to see in the world. One of the ways I see that happening is by gathering women together to support one another. Jean Shinoda Bolen's book *Urgent Message from Mother…Gather the Women, Save the World* is a powerful call for us to extend this invitation to women everywhere.

My workshops and retreats are just one of many opportunities for women to get together and support each other on their spiritual journey. I honor the variety of opportunities presented by many different teachers because each of them offers a different perspective and each of them helps shine a light on our beauty as women. I feel confident that if you attend one of my retreats or workshops you will leave feeling empowered and grateful you came.

For more information, please check out my website **www.maryjwelch.com**.

It's been my privilege to share my story with you. From deep within me, I believe our souls have touched because you have spent your time reading about my life journey. I am very grateful for this oneness of spirit and for the hope it brings to our world.

Namaste,
Mary

Praise for the Retreat

THANK YOU!
THANK YOU!
THANK YOU!
My mind thanks you! My body thanks you! My spirit thanks you! What an amazing retreat! Thank you for bringing forth the courage, wisdom, leadership and intent that allowed all the beautiful goddesses to experience such incredible richness and transformation!
Bonnie

Just what I needed at this point in my life. It was the perfect balance of structured, meaningful group sessions with plenty of free time. I particularly appreciated your respectfulness towards all group members as well as your willingness to go with the flow of group dynamics and "dance with the spirit."
Marilyn

A quick note to say a huge thank-you for the retreat weekend. It was so wonderful!…You are a gift…I appreciate so much your infectious joy, your deep commitment to women, your gentle coaxing…. You are truly a loving presence and I thank you for all of these things.
Pat

…an oasis, but not a mirage, ~ one could drink deeply…I want to thank you for the incredible experience of last weekend. It was truly magical, and I am not the same person I was when the workshop started. You are truly gifted…with creativity, talent, and integrity you led us all to new places and insights. God bless you and this work which is helping to illuminate our world.
Debra

Wisdom Resources

The following books had a profound effect on my life, but by no means is this an exhaustive list. These are the ones that acted as a catalyst in some way for getting me unstuck and moving me forward at different times on my spiritual journey. I am forever grateful to the authors for their insights and their courage in probing the depths.

A Woman's Journey to God - Joan Borysenko

Anatomy of the Spirit - Carolyn Myss

Calling the Circle - Christina Baldwin

Dance of the Dissident Daughter - Sue Monk Kidd

Feelings Buried Alive Never Die - Karol K. Truman

Goddesses In Everywoman - Jean Shinoda Bolen

Godseekers - Earnie Larsen

Leadership and the New Science - Margaret Wheatley

Manifest Your Destiny - Wayne Dyer

Mother Daughter Wisdom - Christiane Northrup

My Mother, Myself - Nancy Friday

Ordinary Enlightenment - John C Robinson

Power of Now - Eckhart Tolle

Sacred Contracts - Carolyn Myss

Secrets of the Millionaire Mind - T. Harv Eker

Seven Spiritual Laws of Success - Deepak Chopra

She, He, We - Robert Johnson

Spiral Dance - Starhawk

The Hidden Messages of Water - Masura Emoto

The Success Principles - Jack Canfield

The Universe is Calling - Eric Butterworth

Tomorrow's God - Neale Donald Walsch

Vibrational Medicine for the 21st Century - Richard Gerber

Women Who Run With The Wolves - Clarissa Pinkola Estes

About the Author

Mary Welch is president of Serend!p!ty Circles, a heart-centered, dynamic, and prosperous business creating programs that enrich lives. She has a degree in Transformational Leadership and is a TOP facilitator. She is a graduate of the Coaches Training Institute and numerous spiritual and personal growth workshops. Mary has been married to her husband Mike for forty years. They live in the Minneapolis area and their three daughters and families live very close by.